Seaside Serenity

By: Brittany Ann Wilson

Seaside Serenity

Low Tide

Sirens Serenade

I wonder what elusive mysteries await beyond the offing,
As the heavens illuminate the evening sky before the dawning.
Do you hear the bewitching sirens Serenade their entrancing melody?
She calls to me, luring me to my fated destiny.
The majestic ocean commences its vast billows,
Clasping me beneath its fathomless shallows.
My lungs overflow with pouring brine blistering my very existence,
Suddenly the temptress reappears to seal her fateful kiss of indulgence.
Never have I savor such divine bliss in my entire being,
Behold! The lost city of Atlantis! Not depleted or deceased but living!
Life evades my solemn lips setting my soul free,
Now I know the secrets of the sea.

Heavens hideaway

Fluffy fleeces roam the infinite wild blue prairie,
Grazing harmoniously obeying sweet lady Mary.
How I yearn to be shrouded by its ivory sheath,
Peering down through the mist to behold angels silver tears beneath.
Do you glimpse within Heavens hideaway to capture me below?
As I gaze above infinitely searching you amongst the earnest rainbow.
I hope you dance admits the whimsical Shepard's of the sky,
Your days abundant with everlasting love as you fly high.
Hence your farewell the most precious jewel has lost its luster,
Swiftly the gentle giants answer the ram horn call of their master.
Unforeseen I noticed the lamb of God cradle you to his kingdom above
on Palm Sunday,
I shall relentlessly endure your gracious memory till we meet again
in heavens hideaway.

Serenity in the storm

The serene seven seas gleam in peace.
At ease in the soothing breeze.
All too still, all too tranquil
The surreal silence screeched more strident than any secret.
Nebulous Neptune arousing from his slumber, extended his trident and bellowed our defeat.
Never in all my years out at sea,
have I laid eyes on such a petrifying beast as the one before me.
Waves of foam crested stallions ascended higher than mighty Goliath himself,
Abruptly they stampede and trample our great vessel... brace yourself!

O Captain, my Captain! How cruel of the high seas to deprive you from my grasp,
With all due haste Davy Jones locker embraced you within its clasp,
Now I'm forever alone out at sea...
Unaware, my nearly annihilated galleon drifts me to the eye of the storm.
How my old life as I knew it will utterly transform.
I cannot, WILL NOT go on without my Captain to guide me to the North Star.
For he is already setting sails afar.

Suddenly in my turmoil, I notice a lone fisherman.
He too beholds me and bellows out, "What's the plan?"
I evade his simple inquiry, for at hand I see our doom.
He chuckled at the notion and replied, "Never assume.
For you cannot make it out alone. Heavens no! Not on one's own.
But, take my hand child, and we will persevere any storm."

I reach for his hand, and instantly I'm blanketed with overwhelming elation.
With Him by my side I am more confident in my relentless motivation.

He vanishes from my sight, yet without doubt I feel his presence by my side.

In Him my faith will abide.

To the omniscient fisherman I beseech for life to refill these empty sails.
In this prayer, the vessel of my belief prevails.
Captain, be my compass, guide me to the light of the North Star.
I transfigure into valiant Jason, conquering the tempestuous sea.
By God's good grace I obtain true peace, and serenity.

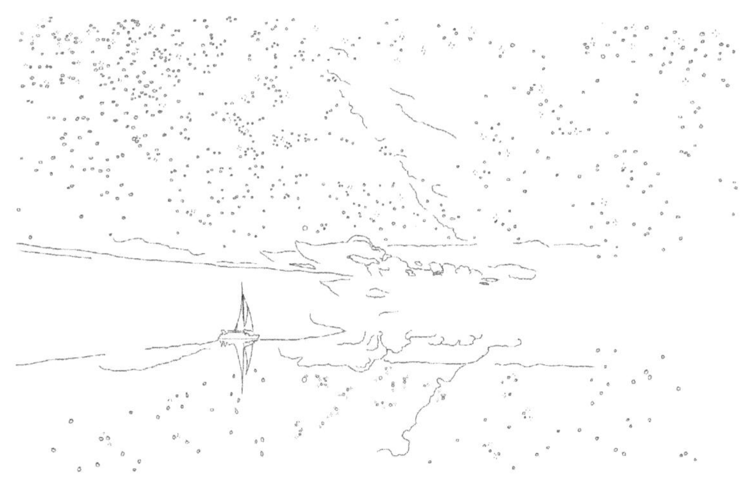

Perpetual Persephone

The morning honey dew trickles down the sweet budding primrose,
As daybreak ascents amongst the barren valleys, breathing life
within the awakening meadows,
Humble feathered creatures recite their gleeful choir for great
Mother Earth's rebirth,
Gaze upon Perpetual Persephone for once again has ascended the
depths of Hades to join her mother's marvelous mirth,
Thus, six enchanted seeds bounded the fated queen, nonetheless no
power on earth can possess a mother and daughters love apart.
Despite deaths inevitable yet implementing final breath of life, can
measure the pure and everlasting love of a mother's heart.

Season of Grace

Heavenly Father,
I aspire to praise.
Not to inquire,
but to give grace
To a compassionate master,
For I am only a humble servant,
Unfit to bare the gifts of a prince;
not even the crumbs due to a peasant,
Yet you renew my life with blessings upon blessings.

I am eternally grateful for my devoted family's unfailing, open arms
with a continual warm embrace,
I am perpetually thankful for my loyal friends whom I also claim to be
my enduring family,
And once more I am lavishly fruitful in gratitude for my internal and
external welfare when far too many souls are not as fortunate,
How can a frivolous fool like me deserve this everlasting grace?
I reminisce in the genuine essence of how Thanksgiving came to be,
oh how it was at first so unlikely,

Therefore, I am ultimately obliged to the great tribal Chieftains of
these lands, to show us clemency, and cultivating our methods in
order to survive.
Henceforth the reminder of the original Thanksgiving, the
descendants of the opening feast will flourish and thrive,

Now, let us acknowledge our bountiful blessings, that we so little
deserve, yet we shall be forever grateful for his amazing grace.

Pretty woman

Pretty woman walking down the street,
Enriched with grace and poise to succeed.
She will never accept defeat.

Mirror, mirror

Mirror, mirror on the wall,
Is everyone waiting to see me fall?
Are they all truly appall?
I don't even dare ask if I'm the fairest of them all,
Every time I behold myself in the mirror,
I can only make out a stranger,
Under one's breath it weakly whispers,
You are a disaster...
You are a failure...
No one appreciates you, not even hereafter,
The invisible man clasps my timid tongue within,
Gasping for air,
Beseeching a prayer,
To only behold my inner demons smirking a toxin grin,
Restless nights,
Breathless frights,
The devil himself is winning my fight,
Upon a fortnight,
My magnificent maker heeded my prayer and sincerely replied,
Don't you worry child,
Simply be reconciled,
And relish that I will never forsake you,
My promise will remain forever true,
Did I not command you to cast all worries upon me to begin anew?
My kingdom above has a plan for you,
Disregard all of Lucifer's deceitful declarations for I have plentiful proposals for you to pursue,

Mirror mirror on the wall,
I am ready for them all,
Let the rainfall,
With God by my side,
I will rise and never fall.

Lost within the chaos

I feel it In the mystifying mist,
The misfortune that does not yet exist,

I hear it in the breeze,
The brewing tempest promptly paving her path to provoke the peace,

But worst of all I bare the sight,
Of the most petrifying fright,

Not the end of mankind,
But the end of humankind,

After all when one relieves his ability to care,
Compassion to share,
Then on is truly lost within the chaos

Sacred Sanctuary

This sacred sanctuary,
Is far from ordinary.

It has aided me against my absolute adversary,
Through my darkest storms that were only temporary.

In my secluded solitary,
I found my prevailing purpose on the contrary.

I will forever carry,
My guardian angels love and memories.
For they were never temporary.
Actually,
Extraordinary,
Just like this sacred sanctuary.

The Reawakening

It all began in a blink of an eye,

After all, it was just another day in paradise.

The alluring aquamarine sky,

Whose serene breeze that brings peace amongst the crashing waves;
the sort that provokes sailors astray to fantasize,

Arise, and be engulfed by the choking, somber smoke.
As if the gray haired sea captain blew out the wax flambeau; thus
with its flickering ambers sparked the infernal flames,

Setting ablaze, The wicked wildfire ignited its uproar and enduringly
out-broke.

Is this how our long exhausted earth finally ends? "Since the
beginning of time", the prophecy proclaims!

I even captured the petrifying sight of the forsaken Blood Moon of
Roanoke,

It's crimson complexion gushed within the baby blue sky, thus casting
chills down my spine.

How eerie the once handsome, now heinous, sun peeked over the
crackling pines,

Diablo hissing his scorching serpentine tongue; licking everything
sacred and full of life,

"You will find no merciful master,"

Admits this damned disaster.

Dear God... My revered raven, Eleanor.

Who unceasingly sought to lend a helping hand thus and so to mentor.

Always availing herself, arising from the shadow.

Prioritizing the children of the forest's needs before her own...
forevermore,

The witty feathered creature perched upon a weathered scarecrow,

Her button eyes filled with sorrowful drops on the verge of downpour.

The once aerie she called home; Devoured by Hades' eternal breath
underneath the crescendo,

Her home is no more.

No more...

Ashes to ashes,

Dust to dust,

Her past life as she knew it abruptly flashes,

before her sight completely changes,

How on God's green earth can anyone adjust?

Eleanor!!

She spreads her Stygian wings off to soar

Into the wrathful woods; she cannot endure!

My suffering soul cries out, "Eleanor!"

"Come back!", I implore
Every second of every day I indefinitely search and explore,
Endlessly searching through the pits of hell,

Please, don't let this be our last farewell.

Without warning, bursting forth from the furious flames, a feathered friend.

Anticipating corvid Elenor e instead to descend,

A Fiery Phoenix,

Rising more vividly than Virile Venus,

She flutters her flaring wings,
Casting a vast draft extinguishing the flames of hell.. a new beginning.
Her beauty and power are beyond overwhelming.

This damned disaster was wiped away from the smooth seashore
The wicked wildfire is no more

Abruptly I attend,

A vague voice that only I can comprehend,

I reminisce this voice from another life, a genuine genius.

"Did I not tell you once before?
I will disclose once more.

Phoenixes burst into flames when it is time for them to die and are reborn from the ashes."

Happiness, can always be found even in the darkness,
'Tis is only the beginning,
The Reawakening.

-For Kayleigh Kirkpatrick

Simple Special Girl

Dreary dreams succumb me to slumber.

I dreamt I appeared in front of a bookcase with a map of Poland above.

I ponder...

Why does this peculiar stairwell feel so familiar?

Is this where she and her family surrender?

As if by natural instinct I reached for the hidden hatch, hence revealing the secret annex.

I paced upon the staircase and eventually discovered the room that belonged to her.

Two small beds, the best little table, uncommonly pretty red shoes, and a wall covered with celebrity, royalty, and artistry.

Curious to impose myself upon the room of a stranger.

Without warning I attend a wan whisper,

"Perhaps we are not so different; instead similar."

Bemused and bewildered that I was not alone,

Could it be the very girl who voiced the diary that is so well known?

I must persevere,

Up the stairwell to that acclaimed attic, I carry on.

And there she was upon the window pane before the evening dawn,

With her dearest diary in hand

In such a way the sweetest smile stretched and screeched out the biggest, "Hello."

"Thank goodness you are not my shadow.

You seem like a friendly fellow.

How do you do?

I am so sorry, this is all so new.

I am not accustomed to company, you see. We are anxiously awaiting for our rescue.

I have faith in the Allies' promise, like the time God promised Noah a rainbow.

Oh how I wish to be free!

Where I can truly be me?

To travel to far distant lands like England and Paris.

Only then will I acquire true bliss, and happiness.

At that precise moment the splendid sparrow perched upon the chestnut tree outside the window,

Ah my dear friend Elpis the Sparrow,

It would only be a shame to confine him below.

He should rejoice however he pleases hereinafter tomorrow.

I could not help but wonder if all along she referred the saintly bird to none other than herself.

At last I wept tender tears for the pure hearted girl, and myself.

That perhaps in another life, we could have been the best of friends,

Why her and not I?

For she encompasses far more innocence.

Abruptly I awaken from my dizzy dream and back into my reality.

In the end, Earth itself endures an epidemic; isolating humanity.

How is it this brave girl lived two years in absolute silence?

Compact and close with other families in a foreign residence.

For her survival.

Yet we are implored to renounce even the most minimal,

For our struggling society's revival.

Nevertheless, we whimper and whine in the appropriate action that is most practical,

But what made this simple girl so special

Was her remarkable refusal

To submit to her imprisonment.

And to seize her moment.

Stalwart Sapling

One must ponder what heaven on earth beholds,
The most magnificent threshold,
Of pure and holy gold,
Oh If one were to hold,

Four abundant headwaters unfold,
Bursting forth, uncontrolled,
Observe The Stalwart sapling upholds,
The prophecy of the tree of life foretold,

Twelve crops of fruit blossom and prosper for the healing of nations,
The initial vow endures, darkness till the end of time extinguish from the heavens,
Eden forever restored for all of God's creations,

The rustling winds whisper beseeching to come forth the ancient tree,
Luminous lattice of leaves canvas the crinkly forest floor; a secret I cannot foresee,
The shimmering sunlight skulk through the slender branches; an ominous voice whispers "The truth will set you free"

My gaze lingers upon the finger like twigs , infinitely reaching out for the light of our Heavenly Father,

Perhaps we are the branches forever linked with the tree of life intertwined as one...

My heart weeps for the children of David, who were deceived by the angel of death thus departed this world light as a feather,

My heart aches for the Indigenous tribes banished from their fathers sacred lands only to voyage upon the trail of tears ;steadily one by one came to be overrun and worn...

My heart deplores for the people of Moses, appropriated from their kingdom thereupon chained against their will to obey a pale master,

Ceaseless scorn
Countless spite
When did all this turmoil begin?
Oh when will it all end?
Brothers and sisters! I implore you to cease this futile hate!
With all due haste don't hold your breath to hesitate,
To love thy neighbor,
And relinquish all hatred thou't harbor,
Allow me to inquire , pose a query...
When pursuing these hateful acts, does one obtain validation?
Any affirmation?
Descendants of Adam and Eve... accompany me to the vitality tree
And let us interlace and radiate God's iridescence integrity

Bittersweet Irony

Isn't that the bitter sweet irony
At our utmost lowest
Brings out
Our empathetic emotion
Our perspiring passion
To write with our hearts what our mouths cannot speak
How unique
As hastily our divine drive and devotion
Absorbs us
Escapes us
When peace and serenity
Consumes us

Hallowed Hurricane

Her heart wept with the pouring rain,
Pleading with God to make the pain,
Go away,
She no longer wished to ever love again,
After her precious love was taken for granted, and in vain,
Her mind, body, and soul were past emotionally drained,
If only the rain could wash all of her melancholy tears,
Away,
Abruptly she perceived the howling winds of the catastrophic cyclone,
The gashing gusts pierced upon her ghastly cheeks, asserting her answer.. she was alone
She beheld the sovereign storm approaching her ocean shore,
Her sinew and steadfastness was impossible to ignore,
The high sea waves surpassed and rose higher than the Himalayas before her eyes,
No matter the countless occasions the courageous tides would crash they never ceased to rise again,
And again,
In the pouring rain,
The strident showers streamed down the gentlewoman's face to refresh her memory.
“Remember me,
Mistress of the seven seas
You have long forgotten who you are.
To Self Doubt you have succumbed, and drifted too far.
With this breath of life,
I beseech you to obliterate the deceitful lies and all of their strife,
Come back to me my Sea Queen!
You have been gone far too long, and unseen,
It has always been you, who possessed the puissant power,
To not only persevere, but also devour...
Any misfortune blown in your path,
But always abiding to rise, and rise again no matter the wicked wrath,
Recognize your worth,

and Realize what treasured gifts you provide to this world,
Remember ME,
Mistress of the Sea"

Deep Sleep

Please,

All I want is sleep.

Deep,

Deep,

Everlasting Sleep,

the sort of kind I can slip away from reality,

Where I will no longer weep.

But it all happens too fast when I'm at last awake,

Greeting me

"Good morning,"

The dreadful pain I can no longer take.

Dizzy Dreams

How heavy my dizzy dreams weigh upon my drooping eyelids,
The inescapable stale slumber amplifies with every reluctant blink,
As if zealous Zeus decrees me to bear the world of dreams "No rest,"
he forbids,
Au courant Atlas I transpose, whereas my absolute desire is to do
anything but to think,
Inevitably I am sheathed by the enchanted Golden Fleece,
Finally granted my release,
My internal peace,

What a hopeless fantasy...
Only a beautiful fool to presume she can escape her reality,
No matter how intoxicating and intricate the ecstasy,
This improper and inadmissible illusion will never come to be,

Make it stop!
I can't escape this self-perpetuating suffering,
I'm still helplessly recovering,
Dreading the decision to accepting,
I will never see them again only in my dizzy dreams...
What loathsome lies...
I ought to realize...

Devout Dreamer

She's a devout dreamer,
A tranquil believer.
Her harmonious hope floats upon her steady serene streams,
While getting lost pursuing her divine dreams.

Beauty rest

My precious princess,
Never lose your beauty rest,
Over pointless circumstances thus consumes your magnificent mind
to be stressed,
It's for the absolute best,
And you will be astonishingly blessed.

Sweet Serene Seaside

How pleasantly the playful palm leaves sway in the perfectly
contented ocean air.
Soaking up the stimulating sunshine in sweet serene Seaside without
a worry or a care.
Captivating the peppy melody of the rejuvenating reggae,
"Don't worry,
Be happy"
Left on replay,
Indulging in the heavenly pina coladas,
Or was it the Bff, with its savory bananas?
I can't decide!
I've already tried,
However, absolutely and positively the best way,
Is that fruity concoction, the frosé!
After all, there are no worries in paradise,
I attest,
When the sun sets,
Behind the loyal lighthouse landmark, I have never beheld such
beautiful breathtaking skies.
Although,
We must compromise.
And come to realize,
There may be gloomy and dreary days; even off the coast,
Of sweet sunny Florida.
However, it is in these overcast melancholy moments where it is up to
you, and only you, to make the most

Of this crazy roller coaster we call life, and absorb its euphoria.
Remember honey,
It's only a bad day.
Not a bad life.

Adventure awaits

I'm off on an adventure,

There's no turning back now,

I, and I alone, must take the rocky road to rediscovery and experience The valiant venture.

The fascinating forest embraces me with open arms,

How sudden and strange the secretive sprigs stop to spot and point my next destination with such cryptic charms.

Every now and occasion, the murky mist gently lurks and emerges to cloud my judgement,

It mutters and murmurs under its breath spectral slander

"Worthless"

Abruptly I heed the blood hurling howl from my worst nightmare, my intimate torment,

No .. not today I shall persist and break free from the fiend fog to finally ravish my self enjoyment,

And hold my head up high and higher superior standards,

I am no stranger,
To deadly danger.
I smile and carry on,
Embracing my frightening fears,
Without shedding any tears.
Upon,
The enchanting dawn.

Scintillating Stars

Remember me,
Not for my brief beautiful body,
But for my witty wondrous words,
My smooth silken skin will only wrinkle and wither away,
Yet my warm hearted and inspiring words will forever stay,
Like the shimmering sprinkles of pixie dust scattered across the sable sky,
We curious creatures make out to be scintillating stars,
What makes these sprightly stars so brilliant is long after they die,
They eternally incinerate and illuminate the blank canvas of the galaxy night,
With their cherished light,
And always shine,
Even in the dark empty depths of the unknown,
Don't you see my darling dear,
Long after I am gone from this world,
That is when it will become crystal clear,
Not only was I here,
I left behind,
My unparalleled love,
And my absolute happiness,
Therefore it will perpetually shine,
Till the end of time,
Now And forever will be mine

If Only

If only ...
I can pluck away all of your pitiful pain,
As if a nurturing gardener attending and affirming that no wicked weeds remain,

If only...
I can restore the remembrance roots to your forgotten favorite fuchsia roses,
Instead helplessly bearing witness to the precious pretty pink petals plummet peacefully oblivious to their doomed destructive decomposes,

But most importantly,
If I could just only,
Sodden the forsaken garden,
With the pouring rain,
In hopes,
You will remember me once again

Glass shield

This glass shield,
Placed between you and I,
Might as well been made of solid steel.
Thus to my dismay,
Being so close yet so far away,
Has never felt more surreal.

Not Together

It breaks my heart,
To be kept cruelly apart,
Before you depart,
For pure and peaceful paradise.
When you desperately need our family's love now more than ever,
But to keep you safe amidst this pandemic's grasp, we must not be together.
Oh how I resent this nauseating joke

A Swift and Slow Passing

To leave this world abruptly, and so suddenly,
Or endure the slow suffering?
That is the prevailing question in our own predestined death,
But Not our doomed decision to make.
However, If I were given the choice between the two,
In bidding my final adieu,

For me,
Better swiftly and softly,
To be out of my morose, melancholic misery.
But to spare the pain of my dear family,
A procrastinated and postponed passing,
Offers recourse to wish one last farewell.
For them, I would willingly suffer the inferno of hell.

Hell fires

When it rains,
It pours,
And lord knows,
The hell fires I have endured.

Ebb and Flow

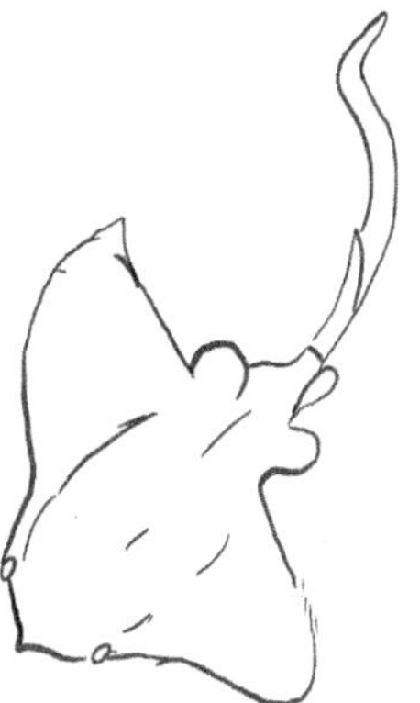

Repeat

Repeat after me
I am worthy
I am worthwhile
I am genuine and gracious
And well deserving of a love
pure
and
precious

Transcendent Throne

After all the spiteful slander,
Is said and done,
Against thy neighbor.
I beseech thee to put down the sinister stone,
We must remind ourselves who truly sits upon the transcendent throne.

Busy Little Honey Bee

Busy little
Honey bee,

Too busy
To notice me,

Sweetly
Studying
Thee,

Are you
Truly free?

My busy little
Honey bee,

Your restless mind
Flutters faster
Than your
Rapid wings,

Hastily humming,

Never halting,

From your,
Pressing hunting,
For the heavenly honey,Don't you see,
My little honey bee,
Not even the sweetest succulent nectar
Or the
amorous ambrosia
hailing from the gods
themselves

Could even begin to compare to the harmonious honey

Within thee,

My little honey bee.

Survivor

I'm a warrior,
Not a worrier...

I'm a fighter,
Not a quitter...

Lastly,
but certainly,
not least,

I'm a survivor.
And,
I Will rise higher,
To vanquish any hell fire.

Stuck

Don't get stuck,
In your own slump.
Know when to put down the shovel,
And pull yourself out of your pensive pit,
Back up to surface level.

Blooming

Keep

Growing

...

Don't stop

Blooming

Loosely Leaves

If
It does not want me,
Then
I do not want it.
Just like the loose leaves,
Hanging carelessly off the willow oak tree.
The weeping willow
Sheds no tears
When it's loose leaves
Fall away
Nor grieves
Over them for not wanting to stay
This wise and wonderful willow oak tree
Yearns only
For sterling sunlight

Autumn Breeze

Within the rustling leaves

The cool crisp

Autumn breeze

Gently whispers to me

“Let it go

And

You will find

Inner peace”
Tis
The season
Of change
For a reason

Oneself

When you
Keep giving
So much
Of
yourself
You only
End up losing
One's self' s

Where I am from

Where the gentle ocean waves rush to meet the seaside sandy shore

Tenderly whispering it's restful roar

Granting inner peace for the lost soul

To serenely explore

And discover

Oneself

Is where I am from.

Believe

Believe
In yourself
As
You
Believe
In shooting stars
The magic is not so far

Beautiful chaos

Beautiful chaos,
She was born to be.

Coiled within her wild wavy mane,
Scribing her destiny in the scintillating stars.
Possessing the power of a hallowed hurricane,
But still gentle as the soft seaside shore.

Her soothing serene siren voice will enrapture your strayed sailor soul,
Craving for more,
Of her sun kissed skin.
Sweet saltwater lips,
With silken satin hips.
But
This divine disaster,
Is her own ruler,
And bows down to no master.

A savage stallion,
Roaming through the vast crazy canyon,
But always one in a million.

Promise me

Promise me,
no empty promises,
only complete honesty.

Never break,
Our treasured trust,
But if that day comes to pass...
Trusting you,
With my agonizing ache,
Will be my greatest mistake.

Precious Pearl

Don't rush perfection,
You can not conceive your prized possession,
Without putting in the time, blood, sweat ,and tears,
Even if it takes timeless years,
Not even the Composed and collected oyster,
Hasten his compelling/careful creation,
Of the precious pearl.

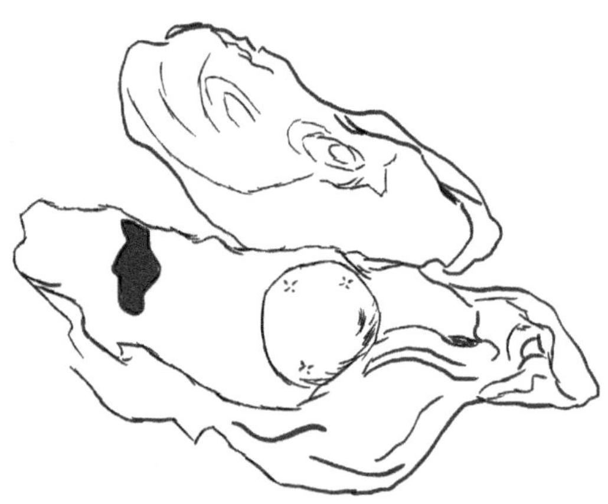

Special Spark

You have that special spark,
To ignite,
Take flight,
And transfigure the impossible,
To precisely THE possible.

Watch Me

When this wicked world snickers at your agony,
Spits at your misery,
And discourteously declares,
"You can't do it."
Glare back and stare,
And shrewdly smile with your reply,
"Watch me."

Looking Back

I was looking back to see,
If
You were looking back to see,
If
I was looking back to see,
That you were looking back at me.

-granddaddy's girl looking back to see her granddaddy

Horizon

Keep an eye
On the
Horizon,
The steadfast sun
Will never stop
Rising.

Sincere Sunrise

This darkness has swallow me whole,
With chaos completely in control,
I fear malicious Monstro lurking,
Waiting,
To swallow my soul,
I worry all hope has escaped me.
But wait...
At last!
I finally see,
The sincere sunrise breaking through,
I never knew
The lustrous light was within me
After all this time

Never

Nothing last forever,

Nor shall this piercing pain,

Never...

Ever

Will it last forever

Simple Sweet Start

It’s a simple sweet start,
To sit back and admire,
With burning desire,
How precious and valuable one truly is
As if Davinci's adored art.

Enough

You are enough,
More than enough,
My diamond in the rough.

Marvelous Magic

She is free
as the seven seas,

Her mermaid soul
Is deeper than the ocean blue,

Her honest heart
Remains forever true,

But,

Her marvelous magic,

Is her persevering passion.

Rip Current

Don't fight the rip current,

You must have courage,

To swim with the flow,

So you will not drown below.

One with the Sea

Be bold,
Be brash,
Be brave,
As the tidal wave,
Set your heart free,
And,
Be one with the sea

Irreplaceable

Your phone
Is
Replaceable

Your car
Is
Replaceable

Your house
Is
Replaceable

But you...
Sweetheart
You are
Irreplaceable

Sinister Stone

Stop throwing sinister stones,

For how much you have grown.

Instead,

Be kind,

To

Your

Wearied mind.

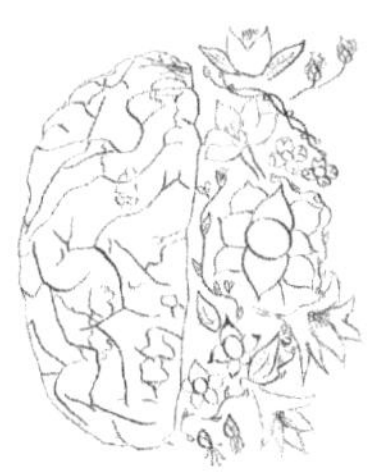

One Step at a time

Sometimes,
We slip up,
And
Dream of giving up.

Sweetheart...
I promise,
It's only a slight setback,
You will get back on track,
One step at a time.
Perhaps,
This cruel calamity was intended to mold
You
Into true gold,
Commencing your climb,
To get up,
And
Rise up,
For your anticipating come up.

The One

Your the one
Who
Survived,
Thrived,
And still
Loves to be alive.

Purpose

Do you hear it?
The bountiful beating,
Prepensely pressing,
Against your consecrated chest?
Feel it
The calm cool air,
Filling up your lungs with care,
With every breath,
Defeating death.
What is it?
...
Purpose
Meaning
A reason
To stay

Between the blank stares

I still see you,
Between the blank stares,
Deep down,
I swear,
I know your still in there,
Somewhere,
Waiting to be seen,
To be heard once again,
To let go of all the pain,

I get carried away,
Remembering,
Our sweet memories,
Refusing,
To let them slip away,
Or you,
Fade away,
Day by day.

I am sorry

I am sorry,
For always apologizing,
Requesting
And
Pleading,
For forgiveness of an unknown sin,
I haven't even committed to begin.

Ceaseless Change

Life,

Is brutally honest.

It has one pure promise,

That remains forever constant,

And that is,

Ceaseless change.

Plans of Prosper

Change,
At first might feel,
Awkward,
Eerie,
And strange.
But,
In exchange,
It is only preparing,
For new beginnings.
That are,
Bigger
And
Better,
Than
Ever
Before.
Plans to prosper,
Not to
Wear and tear
Your surviving soul.

Little do you know

Little do you know,
The trials and tribulations,
You have endure,
Were put in place to ensure,
How far you will grow.

Broken

Can't be fixed
Broken
Left defeated
With my shattered pieces
...
Darling
Your crumbling cracks
Will be built back
Woven with devotion
Into God's beautiful creation
He always intended for you
To mold into

Jubilant June

The complacent caterpillar contemplated on conceiving and
constructing its capricious cocoon,
He knew too well once he crafted his wonderful warm womb,
He wouldn't dream of escaping the encasing to only expose his
weeping wound,
But
He was oblivious of the magnificent Magic that came from deserting
his terrible tomb,
To only emerge as a beautiful butterfly,
spreading his wonderful wings to fly,
In the full moon
Of
Jubilant June.

Rising Tide

Hidden blessing

Set up sufficient space,
For God's amazing grace.
Make requisite room,
To begin your budding bloom.
You have to remove,
The nonessential negativity,
The no good clutter,
Of the false lover,
And the enemies undercover,
In order to improve,
Your peace of mind and place.
Stop the stressing,
Heaven,
Has a hidden blessing.

Backwards and Forwards

One small step backwards,
For
A giant leap forward,
Towards,
Your reward.

Glorious hands

It never fails,
When I helplessly plan.
It crumbles apart like the white sands of time
before it even began.
Time and time again.
I have lost control,
Of my solemn soul.
Pieces missing; no longer whole,
Frightfully beholding it fall below to the bottom barren blackhole.
Lord I beseech you!
You are in control,
Of this lost gypsy soul.
You have always been in charge and in command.
I have failed to understand,
Heaven above has always bigger tidings in planned.
Everything has always resided in your glorious hands.

Darkness

You shine
Your brightest,
In the darkness.

Now and Here

As another year,
Draws to a near,
I shall not shed a sobbing tear,
Or wince at my dooming fear.
I will remain present,
In the
Now
And
Here,
To cherish my life ever so dear.

Hope

Hope,
Is what sews back the strings,
To our broken wings.

Medication

Meditation
Is the best
Medication.

Keep writing

Keep writing;
Never stop fighting
For what keeps your heart beating
Love, art, and beauty,
Grants us mere mortals understanding,
And
Meaning,
To our precious life.

The Sandy Surface

One with a pure purpose,
Is quite far from worthless.
There is always more to be discovered beneath The Sandy Surface.

Heart of Gold

A heart of gold,
Is breathtaking beautiful to behold.
So I am told.
It does not grow cold,
From the harsh hands that sinisterly scold,
It's marvelous mold.
No...
One who possesses a good heart,
Could never dream of hurting someone without inflicting pain onto themselves.
And for that is what defies and sets the two apart.

Just like magic

And just like magic,
Before you even know it.
In a blink of an eye,
When life passes by.
To a snap of a finger undoing your deep slumber of a hazy hypnosis,
You won't even notice,
Your moving on
To
Bigger
And
Better
Blessings.

Saving Salvation

I fully believe with my entire being,
That God will never give you more than you can endure,
My mighty warrior.
He will never let a sacred soul suffer
While he is in control.

He heard the conversations you did not hear.
At first it may not be clear,
Between the blurry tears.
But do not fear.
What he removes,
He not only replaces,
But improves,
The dreary devastation,
With a worthier destination,
Your saving salvation.

When life gives you pineapples

When life gives you pineapples,
...make pina coladas

You are…

You are
The bushwacker
To my
Bff

What does the BFF mean?

What does the bff mean?
Does it really mean best friends forever?
Or bushwhackers frose and frozen drinks?
Either one the bff means many meanings
I am asked this on a daily routine.
Sometimes it is not so easy to see between
The serene scene
Or seasides grassy green
While your on vacation time,
But sometimes
Every now and then,
You can witness it first hand in action.
Shared in these happy occasions
While in sweet paradise.
And it all started in that lil metal tent
Where it was never meant
Or intent
To take off with such a hit.
All my blood sweat tears and sacrifice,
Was all worth it to pay the precious price.
During my dismal darkness,
From someone's else's selfishness,
Brought out my beautiful brightness.
Thus with this act of caring compassion,
In hopes it will cause a chain reaction,
In spreading the same love, kindness, and happiness,
Will more than suffice,
For this bff.
...
And that is what the bff means
My jelly bean.

Marvelously Mine

Rain
Or
Shine,
I will seize
The day,
And
Make it
Marvelously Mine.

Grief

Grief...
Is never brief.
It is a treacherous thief,
Of one's beautiful belief.
...

This perpetual pain,
Is what poor souls pray,
To never endure again.
Begging,
Pleading,
No
Groveling,
To stay away,
And never come back for the rest of one's dreadful days.

The oppressive overthinking,
Is the significant source of my shameful shrinking.

I am...
Withering away,
Spiraling down my slippery sway.
Wondering what I weigh?...
Unwillingly,
Developing,
My obstinate disorder...
What troubled torture.

I must honor,
My granddads granddaughter,
By taking back control of my uneasy emotion,
For my magical motion.
At long last my anxious anxiety,
Was no longer mine to worry.

I was tensely thinner,
Sickly skinnier,
But I had to look inner.
Yes I grew smaller,
But I am no goner...
This destructive disorder,
Will not get the best of me.
That I can guarantee.
I am stronger,
And wiser,
Than ever before.
Hear me roar.

Too much yet never enough

Sweetheart,
While you were perniciously told you were too much for others,
You were never.
You are so much,
And magnificently more.

Priceless

Money is momentary,
Therefore worthless.
I'm here for the magical moments,
That lights a special spark in one's eye and reminds them who they are on the inside.
Brightening people's glooming day,
By being a radiant ray
In sunny Florida today
And every day.
Because
The memories made,
With families and bff alike,
In serene seaside
Will never fade.
...
And that is priceless.

All Day Everyday

I'm dreaming
Seeing
believing
in threes
I'm living
breathing
And
Cruising
down the streets
On 30a
Working away
At the bff
In the USA
Three bff
Miss
Amanda
Audrey
And I

Who am I
I'm the og
Brittany the bff
It's all in the b
How do you do what you do?
Because no matter what
Rain or shine
I give it all to him
All day everyday

The b
In the
Bff

I have to take care of me,
Before I can take care of the big b.
I am not my machines,
By any means.
I am just a human being.

Keep The Fire Burning

Keep the fire burning.
No tears,
My darling dear.
You can't burn wet wood,
Understood?

I know you dream of me returning,
Walking through the panned door.
Remembering more than how I left this ephemeral earth before.
Wiping away your troubled tears,
But baby girl I have always been here.
Heeding to every pious prayer.
Listening to all of the astonishing accounts of how the bff came to be,
Living your best life by the serene sea,
And spreading the word of God just like King G.
Because
You were born free.

...

Remember who you are,
And how far,
the North Star
and
you
have come.
Your granddaddy's girl,
Mimi's world,
Our perfect Pearl.

The same ferocious fire,
That kindles your grandparent's driven desire.
Is passionate perseverance,
To go the difficult demanding distance.

Roy boy
too was continuously
And
Constantly,
Criticize
And
Chastise
"Your piss poor,
You live on a dirt floor!
Damn dumb!
Ain't going nowhere Roy!
Now get back to picking the cotton field white boy!"
But he too,
Had the same damn stubbornness,
Steadfastness,
And relentless
Heart of a decisive donkey
And never gave up,
And became King G,
Living the American dream,
On top of his hill,
Strong willed,
Off of Tiffany lane.
No pain,
No gain.
Is the life game.
So let it rain,
Again
And
Again,
Healing the grieving pain,
Of the Gillespie family that remains.
I have taught you everything I know
And
Look how far you have come to grow
And learn so much more.
Keep writing my Jane Austen,

Keep learning my history girl,
And never stop growing my splendid sunflower.
You have always had the same persevering power,
My wildflower.
You know what to do
Keep the fire burning,
Never stop glowing.

I'll Be Back

"I came through and I shall return."
Vowed MacArthur.
Although he was left with no choice but to retreat,
He did not accept defeat.
2 drawn out distressing years in the pitiless pacific seas,
MacArthur took back the Philippines from the Japanese.
This reward with adoration and admiration,
The high homage one could only hope to receive,
Best believe,
The Medal of Honor.
For fulfilling the valiant promise,
Of defending the lives of those who could not defend themselves
against a malevolent tyrant.
My grandfather
Applauded
MacArthur
Like no other.
I glimpse back,
To wish one last farewell,
My eyes start to swell,
On the slight setback,
Of letting go,
the house that built me.
My mind begins to dwell,
Of all the magical moments made,
In granddaddy's house.
Suddenly
My smile brightens my solemn spirit,
I would much rather inherit,
The time
Memories
And stories
Rather than
The momentary materials.
My granddad's house lives forever within me.

This is no goodbye.
No time to cry.
My eyes are dry.
And
I'll be back
To take back
The pride
Of the
Proud pack.

Great Generation

It's up to our great Generation,
To heal our divided nation,
And make the human connection.
All it takes is one act of compassion to start a chain reaction.
A time of reflection
Of our imperfections
Is needed
Now more than ever
Alarming attention
And
Careful consideration
For the destruction of others education
Communication
But most of all freedom..
Is the most devastating depression of affliction
An offensive Oppression

A time of gratification,
For our perspiring protection,
From the steadfast soldiers,
Who bear a heavy burden on their shoulders.
Not all heroes wear cape
Giving their lives on the line for the sacrifice,
Will more than suffice,
They never laid down their lives for a price.
And that's something money can never buy.
It's priceless
To be in paradise
Therefor
A monumental memorial occasion,
When the flag rises
On the horizon
It's a small token to pay homage for our fallen brothers and sisters
I believe a commemorative celebration.
Is more than at hand

Equality,
And
Liberty,
For all
Lastly,
Honesty,
In authority.
Is why
We are
Proud
To be
An
American

Fairy Godmother

Fairy Godmother always knew,
When I was sad and blue,
On days that reminded me of you,
Or when rumors in our kingdom flew,
That simply were not true.
Thus intended to break me in two.
But she knew,
How true,
My honest heart pushes and pours,
Forevermore,
For the truth to endure.
Bibbidi bobbidi boo!
Just like magic she appeared out of the blue,
With a wave of her magnificent magical wand,
My courage grew,
With sparking red shoes,
And I would feel anew.
I felt compelled within myself to thank her for believing in me,
To see the puissant power within thyself to set me free.
When no one else had faith, trust or pixie dust.
Shhh shhh shh,
She places her gentle soft fingers on my cherry lips and says
"No need to respond,
Sweet pea princess I see beyond,
You must carry on.
When I am long gone.
Upon the early dawn,
You will carry our torch,
Never to scorch.
bearing our beguiling beacon,
For the bold
The brave
And beautiful bff.
By placing others before yourself,
Teamwork makes the dream work.

Fairness and kindness walk hand in hand.
Lastly
But certainly
Not least,
Believe in Brittany the bff."

Thank you fairy Godmother,
For always having faith trust and pixie dust in me.

- For Heather Baxter

The pink drink and The flower power

The pink drink and its flower power,
At the bff we frose all day every day,
And Without doubt I piously pray,
For every woman to recognize her celestial worth,
While momentarily visiting this materialistic earth.
A pretty flower,
For a pretty lady.
Milady,
Your beautiful blossom was precious and precisely placed to enduringly empower,
For Every wonderful woman .
A friendly reminder,
She is a heavenly divine creation.
Worthy of celebration.
Because
Gods beautiful creations,
Are more than worthy of admiration.

Compiling Compass

It's not what you know
It's WHO you know

Connections
Are often times our
Directions

We form our essential encompass
For Our compiling compass

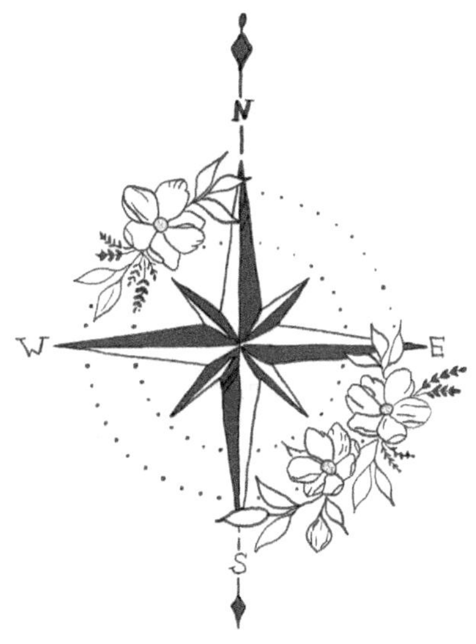

Not all hero's wear capes

Not all hero's wear capes.
Every now and then
One must take a sweet escape
Before anything fragile, or worth of value breaks,
Disappear like Harry Houdini,
It's that simple and easy.
As if granting wishes like a graceful genie.
From dusk till Dawn.
The spectacular show must go on.
Whatever it takes
After all,
When we stumble and fall,
We pick ourselves right back up buttercup.

Soaring Sea

By the soaring Sea,

My heart is filled with glee.

Thus my sacred soul is set free.

Radiant Role Model

Why keep your controlled chaos bottle?
While you can lead through example and action?
Be a radiant role model,
A natural inspiration
With no limitation.
I refuse to receive the Medal of Honor.
Instead
I prefer the term grateful gardener,
A natural nurturer,
So to speak
Therefore I can continue to grow
My grand goals
By taking control
Of my once lost soul.

Ocean child

Stay wild,

Ocean child.

Be true,

To you,

When setting sails through,

The deep desolate blue.

You will return to shore to rediscover who you genuinely are,

May the North Star

Guide you

When you stray too far.

Don't be afraid,

To begin anew.

www.ingramcontent.com/pod-product-compliance
Lightning Source LLC
LaVergne TN
LVHW012112160826
845678LV00014B/3048

9798419473805